GERMAN INFLUENCE
IN AMERICAN EDUCATION
AND CULTURE

German Influence
in American Education
and Culture

By

JOHN ALBRECHT WALZ

Select Bibliographies Reprint Series

 BOOKS FOR LIBRARIES PRESS
FREEPORT, NEW YORK

First Published 1936
Reprinted 1969

LA
205
W3
1969

STANDARD BOOK NUMBER:
8369-5101-8

LIBRARY OF CONGRESS CATALOG CARD NUMBER:
70-99672

PRINTED IN THE UNITED STATES OF AMERICA

☆

» » THE substance of this paper was presented in the form of a lecture at a Round Table on "American-German Relations" held in connection with the *Institute of Public Affairs* at the University of Virginia, Charlottesville, Virginia, from July 8th to July 13th, 1935.

$\mathcal{G}$ERMAN literature in modern times was slower in attaining distinction than either English or French literature. The religious wars in the wake of the Reformation culminating in the destructive Thirty Years' War put German culture and intellectual life definitely behind that of the Western nations. In all matters pertaining to literature, intellectual refinement and progress the Germans were not taken seriously by the English or the French during the seventeenth and early eighteenth centuries. But from the middle of the eighteenth century on we witness an astonishing development of German literature and culture which, by the end of the century, put Germany at the head of European nations in things of the spirit and intellect. The epoch is marked by the appearance of the first three cantos of Klopstock's *Messias* in 1748 and of Goethe's *Faust* in 1808, the greatest work of poetry since the dramas of Shakespeare. This new richness of German life was not recognized abroad for some time. The German language was little known outside of Central Europe and foreigners were not accustomed to look to Germany for intellectual inspiration. There is only one German literary work that made its way throughout the civilized world during the last quarter of the eighteenth century: *The Sorrows of Young Werther,* which Goethe published in 1774. It is the first German book that in an English translation was extensively read in the United States, arousing here as elsewhere the admiration of the young and the condemnation of the old and the conservative. The home of George Washington, Mount Vernon, harbors to this day a picture representing an incident from *Werther's Sorrows,* an indication of the popularity of the book in the young republic.

The new Germany of thought and culture was discovered and proclaimed to the world by a French woman, Madame de Staël. This brilliant woman traveled in Germany in the early nineteenth century, visiting Weimar and other centers of intellectual life. In 1813 her book, *De l'Allemagne,* appeared, in which she gave an account of her studies and observations in Germany. The book was at once translated into English, and a reprint of the English translation appeared in New York in 1814. With this American reprint the influence of German thought on American life and education may be said to have begun.

All through the eighteenth century there were thriving German settlements in Pennsylvania where the German language flourished, but the Pennsylvania Germans were not in touch with the new intellectual currents of their old homeland, hence they were not mediators between the intellectual life of Germany and that of the United States. The Pennsylvania Germans were for the most part deeply religious. The Bible and the Church supplied their intellectual needs. They have the distinction of having issued the first Bible in the United States—the German Bible printed by Christopher Sauer in Germantown[1] in 1743—while the English settlers imported their Bibles from England. They have played an important part in the history of religious movements in the United States, but they did not transmit the intellectual thought of Germany to their English-speaking fellow citizens.

Madame de Staël's book on Germany gave an appreciative account of the work of the great German poets and thinkers—Lessing, Herder, Goethe, Schiller, and others—and of the new German idealistic philosophy. It also contained a short chapter on German universities, which the author calls the most learned universities in Europe. It gave an account of the new education in Germany brought about by the adoption of the system of Pestalozzi, which Madame de Staël considered far superior to the educational teaching of

Rousseau because it was practical and adaptable to all children in contrast with the lack of these qualities in Rousseau's ideas. Rousseau had clearly seen the faults of the old system, but the remedy he proposed was, in her opinion, worse than the evil he wished to cure. It was fantastic and did not admit of practical application.

Madame de Staël's book has been called the discovery of a new continent of intellectual and spiritual ideas. In France, England and the United States it aroused an eagerness to know more about these German ideas. George Ticknor, the famous Spanish scholar at Harvard, tells us in his journal that the reading of *De l'Allemagne* first gave him the desire to study at a German university. Emerson read the book, as did Edward Everett, Margaret Fuller, George Bancroft. We find many references to it in American literature of the early nineteenth century. Inspired by this book, a number of young Americans, all of whom attained distinction in later life, decided to go to Germany to study. Edward Everett went to Göttingen in 1815; George Ticknor, George Bancroft, Joseph G. Coggswell followed. John Lothrop Motley studied in Göttingen from 1831-33, later in Berlin.[2] They form the vanguard of that host of Americans who have since gone to study at German universities down to the second decade of the twentieth century.

An interest was awakened in the study of the German language as a part of collegiate education. Harvard College and the University of Virginia were the first American universities to introduce the study of German. Thomas Jefferson, whose large mind always looked toward the future, believed that the study of modern languages should form a part of American higher education and therefore also a part of the curriculum of his newly founded university. Among the professors that he engaged in England was a German scholar, Dr. Blaettermann, who as Professor of Modern Languages gave the first instruction in the German language at the University of Virginia. That was in 1825, the first year that the university was in session.[3] In the same year Harvard College appointed Charles Follen as instructor in German.[4] Follen had all the German idealism of that day, though he was a fugitive from political oppression. In 1830 he was made Professor of German. The fund which supported the professorship had been given by personal friends for five years. As at the end of that period the fund was not renewed, Charles Follen, in spite of distinguished service, had to sever his connection with Harvard College.

It should be mentioned, however, that the Public Academy of the City of Philadelphia, later called the Public College of the City of Philadelphia, founded in 1749, had German instruction. This institution was transformed into the University of Pennsylvania in 1779. Through the influence of two Pennsylvania German trustees there was appointed in 1780 a German professor of philology, who was to give instruction in Latin and Greek in the German language. The German Institute, as the German department was called, was very prosperous for a few years. It had at one time as many as sixty students, but interest soon waned and it was discontinued in 1787.[5] Columbia College in New York also had German instruction during the eighteenth century from 1784 to 1795, when it was discontinued. German was not taken up again until 1830.[6]

German ideas did not influence the American colleges at first, but rather the common schools and the education of the masses. The American public-school system appears to us to-day so impressive, taken as a whole it is so well organized and so thoroughly American that we cannot see any foreign influence, least of all German influence, yet American public-school men in the nineteenth century were well aware of the great debt they owed to the German schools.

Burke A. Hinsdale, who for many years held the chair of the Science and the Art of Teaching in the University of Michigan, says in his book on *Horace Mann and the Common School Revival in the United States* (New York, 1913, p. 61): "It is Germany that, in this century, has exerted upon our country the most protracted, the deepest and the most salutary educational influence." Two other American writers on education, C. H. Hoyt and R. C. Ford, in their biography of John D. Pierce,[7] the first superintendent of public schools in the State of Michigan, express a similar view: "It would be a difficult task to give any kind of a just estimate of the extent or value of German influence upon American education, in the organization of school systems, in the modification of those already established, and in the reform of courses of study and methods of teaching."

In the early nineteenth century the German States, especially Prussia, had thoroughly reorganized and modernized their schools to give all the people, rich and poor, intellectual and moral training. It was the idealistic spirit of German classicism, Kant's and Fichte's moral teachings which, together with the devastating effects of the Napoleonic wars, induced the paternal governments of the German States to build up a system of popular education that would raise the moral and intellectual level of the whole people. The University of Berlin had been founded by the Prussian Government in 1810 with the avowed intention of retrieving in the realm of the spirit and the intellect what Prussia had lost in physical power.[8] Politically, Prussia did not become a free country, but its ruler felt the obligation, as the supposed father of his people, to care for the proper education of his subjects. We observe then what is characteristic of German conditions throughout the nineteenth century and what is perhaps unique in German history—the lack of certain political rights and liberties combined with the greatest intellectual and spiritual freedom and progress. It was this lack of political liberty which for many Americans formed the strongest argument against the adoption of Prussian methods and ideas of education.

But other European countries were also dissatisfied with the traditional methods of education; in fact, the early nineteenth century shows everywhere an intense interest in educational matters and in educational reform. In 1830, the French Government sent the distinguished scholar and philosopher, Victor Cousin, to Germany to study the school system of the German States, especially Prussia. Cousin was singularly fitted for this mission. He had lived in Germany and had studied German philosophy, he was a personal friend of men like Hegel and Schelling. He had an understanding of things German as was possessed by but few foreigners. In 1832 he published in two volumes a report of his observations and impressions entitled: *Rapport sur l'état de l'instruction publique dans quelques pays de l'Allemagne, et particulièrement en Prusse.* Again it was a French book that announced to the world the progress Germany had made. The book proved a sensation. In 1834 the part pertaining to the Prussian primary schools was translated into English by Sarah Austin and published at London with the title: *Report on the State of Public Instruction in Prussia.* In her preface (p. xxii) Mrs. Austin "entreats" the reader "never to lose sight of the fact that what is here laid before him . . . is still only a part of the whole, and that it is as a whole that the national education of Prussia is so peculiarly worthy of admiration and of study."

Mrs. Austin's translation was republished in New York in 1835 with a preface by the American educator, J. Orville Taylor. In this preface Taylor says that the volume should be welcomed by every American citizen. "Many parts of this system of public instruction are not adapted to the spirit and feelings of the American people, nor to their form of government. Yet from the results of this great experiment in giving the *whole people* that *kind* and *degree* of instruction which they need, some of the most useful and practical lessons may be obtained. The nature and operations of the mind are the same in all countries, and the relations which exist between knowledge and the intellectual and moral faculties, remain unchanged under every system of instruction and every form of government" (p. v).

Taylor in this preface used the expression "normal school," which he says is the Prussian name (p. xi), but "normal school" (*i. e.,* Normalschule) has never been used in German, it is the French name *école normale* which Cousin had used in his *Report* as the name for teachers' seminary.

Taylor points out the great difference between the spirit of American civil government and that prevailing in Prussia and Germany, but in his opinion that should not prevent Americans from benefiting by the example set by Prussia. Cousin had made the same point. The fact that the Prussian government is an absolute government in no way vitiates the value of the "excellent" law on education adopted in 1819. "It is impossible not to be struck with its profound wisdom. . . . It is a king, and an absolute king, who issued this law; it is an irresponsible minister who advised or who digested it; and yet we find no injudicious spirit of centralization or of official despotism." (Ed. New York, 1835, p. 106.)

Nor has Cousin any patience with Frenchmen who might object to the Prussian system of education on patriotic or national grounds. "The experience of Germany, and particularly of Prussia, ought not to be lost upon us. National rivalries or antipathies would here be completely out of place. The true greatness of a people does not consist in borrowing nothing from others, but in borrowing from all whatever is good, and in perfecting whatever it appropriates." (*ibid.*, p. 292.)

In Ohio, which was rapidly increasing in wealth and population, the question of the reform and extension of the public school system occupied the attention of the best citizens of the State. In 1836 Calvin E. Stowe, professor at Lane Theological Seminary in Cincinnati, husband of Harriet Beecher Stowe, delivered a lecture before the Convention of Teachers at Columbus which was shortly afterward published with the title, *The Prussian System of Public Instruction and Its Applicability to the United States* (Cincinnati, 1836). In one of the recommendations prefixed to the lecture we find the statement: "The truths brought out by Professor Stowe shall rescue this nation from the reproachful superiority of the monarchies and despotisms of Europe, and secure to our republic the triumphs of universal education." A copy of the discourse was sent by the Governor of the State to the General Assembly for their consideration. In the preface (p. xiv) Professor Stowe says that he is indebted for the facts to Cousin's *Report* and to certain articles in the *Conversations-Lexicon.* "The wisdom and benevolence of the admirable system render it well worthy of the attentive consideration of every friend of the human race; and it cannot fail to be useful to the enlightened and patriotic citizens of Ohio and the other western states, who are now laboring with so praiseworthy zeal in the cause of education." The lecture opens with the sentence: "The Kingdom of Prussia, at the present time, affords the rare spectacle of an absolute sovereign exerting all his power for the intelligence and moral improvement of his people. The government of Prussia, in which the voice of the king is everything and the voice of the people nothing, does more for the education of the whole people than has ever been done by any other government on earth." The lecture gives the clearest and the most succinct account of the Prussian school system to be found in American literature of the time. At the end the author summarizes

eighteen

his impressions: "It is impossible to contemplate the system without admiring the completeness and beauty of the plan—the wisdom, benevolence and good taste of its minutest regulations—and the promptness and efficiency with which every part of it is carried into execution." (P. 49.)

The second part of the lecture bears the title: *Applicability of the Prussian System to the United States* (pp. 50-80). Changes must be made slowly, the people must be prepared and educated for these changes, but the public men of Ohio have shown their readiness to further this good work. The Governor of Ohio, in a recent message, "called the legislative attention to the Prussian school system" (p. 55). More must be left to popular action, to the free choice of the community. Few, if any, of the Prussian laws can be adopted without some modification. But Stowe enumerates eight characteristics of the Prussian system which deserve to be adopted in the United States, the most important being the recognition of the duty and obligation of every citizen to educate his children, just as it is his duty to bear arms in defense of his country; the proper training of teachers, which presupposes the establishment of institutions for their training; extensive and thorough instruction, proper supervision, and as an improvement on the Prussian system he recommends the establishment of district libraries for the use of both pupils and teachers. The German school libraries are intended for the teachers and are of little benefit to the pupils.

In the same year Professor Stowe was commissioned by Governor Lucas of Ohio, at the request of the General Assembly of the State, to examine the European school system during a contemplated tour in Europe and to make a report on it. The report was presented in December, 1837. The greater part deals with the German primary schools, in which Stowe was chiefly interested. It was printed by order of the Legislature of Ohio and copies were sent to every school district in the State. It was reprinted in Boston by order of the House of Representatives of the Legislature of Massachusetts, March 29, 1833. It was also reprinted in New York, Pennsylvania, and several other states.[9]

Stowe gives a detailed account of actual lessons he attended in the schools of Württemberg and Prussia. Only in the lessons in arithmetic could he find no substantial improvement over the methods prevailing in the best American schools. (P. 38, ed. Boston, 1833.) He considers the system "in its great outlines, as nearly complete as human ingenuity and skill can make it; though undoubtedly some of its arrangements and details admit of improvement; and some changes will of course be necessary in adapting it to the circumstances of different countries" (p. 52). He is impressed with the fact that singing and drawing are taught in all the primary schools. The objection that the introduction of so extensive and complete a course of study into American common schools was a visionary idea and could never be realized he meets by saying that he has not presented a theory but a fact, a copy of actual practice. "If it can be done in Europe, I believe it can be done in the United States; if it can be done in Prussia, I know it can be done in Ohio. The people have but to say the word and provide the means, and the thing is accomplished" (p. 53). The first requirement is to have competent teachers. Teachers must be trained for their profession, for teaching should be a profession like law and medicine. To accomplish that there must be teachers' seminaries as in Germany.

In 1835 George S. Hillard, a well-known lawyer and writer in Boston, read before the American Institute of Instruction, an organization of teachers, a lecture prepared by Miss Eliza Robbins, which was published in book form at Philadelphia the following year with the title, *Lecture on Public Instruction in Prussia.* It is largely based on Cousin's Report on the

Prussian schools. "The spirit rather than the details of this great institution is applicable in the United States," the author states at the very beginning of the lecture. Two striking features of the Prussian system are pointed out: "the respect felt by the nation for the dignity and uses of education; and the positive fitness required by the laws for the exercise of the respective duties of those employed in the administration of it." (P. 8.) "Can the Prussian mode of education be applied to this country?" the lecturer asks (p. 51). "It has been adopted in France, by recommendation of Cousin, but not without national modification. We may not be able to adopt its whole economy, it may not be desirable to us, but as teachers of the young we can follow its suggestions, for it requires the word of legislation to order its operation. But there are three elements of power in the Prussian system which should be adopted in this country: wise supervision, qualified teachers, and rational school-books." (Pp. 54, 57.)

When Girard College was founded in Philadelphia in 1836 the trustees decided to send Alexander D. Bache, who had just been elected president, to Europe to study for two years the educational systems of the European countries before entering upon active work at the college. Bache visited schools and institutions

in Great Britain, Germany, Holland, France, Austria,
Switzerland. After his return he published in 1839
an extensive report of 666 pages giving a description
of the schools he had visited.[10] More than one-third
of the work is devoted to the schools of the German
states. Of the Prussian system of primary schools he
says (p. 171): "This is the most perfect of the cen-
tralized systems, allowing considerable latitude in the
arrangement of the individual schools, while all are
subject to the influence of the central authority. Its
present condition is the result of experience, and thus
it commends itself to enlightened imitation, by which
I mean that which, laying aside what is inapplicable
to the political or social institutions of the country
adopting it, would employ the large amount of useful
material which it contains. The schools contain much
more than is applicable to our country than the system in general." . . . "The higher class of primary
schools seem to me in better condition than those of
any other of the larger European states." (P. 172.)
As to the instruction in the primary schools he says:
"The subjects of popular instruction are excellent in
themselves and the methods of teaching are in general
the most improved. Prussia has certainly set a noble
example in this respect. It is true that the government has provided that the incidentals of instruction,

which exert so strong an influence on the mind, shall all tend to educate the people in sentiments of attachment to the existing order of things, but they would have been untrue to their political system had they not done so, and this fact instead of leading to a rejection of the experience of their schools by nations more advanced in the true principles of government, should stimulate them to a like care in their systems of education." (P. 230.) Of the Prussian teachers he says that he found among them more instances of ardent attachment and devotion to their profession than in any other country he visited (p. 131).

In Massachusetts the public schools of the State in the early nineteenth century had not kept pace with the general progress of society. They had remained stationary, which, when the new movement set in, meant retrogression. Francis Bowen, professor of moral philosophy at Harvard, characterized the common school system of New England before the Common School Revival with the words: "It had degenerated into routine, it was starved by parsimony. Any hovel would answer for a school-house, any primer would do for a text-book, any farmer's apprentice was competent to 'keep school'." The American reprint of Cousin's Report he calls "a judicious and timely step, as the work contained the outlines, and even the minute details, of the most elaborate and complete system of common schools which had yet been devised in the civilized world." [11]

There was a lack of trained teachers and that was universally felt to be the chief cause of the decline of the public schools. Private schools had sprung up in large numbers and were patronized by the better class of citizens. The need of the training of teachers had been pointed out by men like James G. Carter, Thomas H. Gallaudet in Connecticut, and others, feeble attempts had been made to establish private training schools, but no model for such training existed.[12] It was Charles Brooks (1795-1872),[13] a clergyman at Hingham, who called attention to the German seminaries for teachers and finally succeeded in getting such a training school established in Massachusetts. It was the first state normal school. Brooks late in life (1864) gave an account of his work for the normal schools in Massachusetts in a lecture to which he gave the curious title: "History of the Missionary Agency, in Massachusetts, of the State Normal Schools of Prussia, in 1835, '36, '37 and '38." The lecture was delivered at the "Quarter Centennial Normal-School Celebration" in Framingham, Mass., July 1, 1864 and "printed by request, not published," Boston, 1864.

"To the Prussian system of State Normal Schools belongs the distinctive glory of this day," we are told almost at the beginning of the lecture. Brooks' account is succinct and to the point. In 1834 he met in London a German official, Dr. H. Julius of Hamburg[14] who was on his way to the United States, having been sent by the King of Prussia to study the conditions of American schools, hospitals, prisons and other public institutions. They took ship together and on the voyage of forty-one days Dr. Julius explained to Charles Brooks the Prussian system of elementary education. "I fell in love with the Prussian system," Brooks says, "and it seemed to possess me like a missionary angel. I gave myself to it; and in the Gulf Stream I resolved to *do* something about *State* Normal Schools." "When the doctor came to visit me at Hingham, I told him I had been studying the Prussian system for six months, and that I felt called of God to try and introduce it into my native state." Dr. Julius "consented to give an account of the Prussian system before the Committee on Education in our legislature. His delineations were clear and judicious, but so brief as led to no action."

"Much depended on the right beginning," Brooks continues. "I knew that the common people would be more moved by one practical fact than by a bushel of metaphysics. I therefore wrote three enormously long lectures; namely, two hours each. In the first I described minutely the Prussian State system, its studies, books, classifications, modes of teaching, government, rewards, punishments, etc.; a perfect catalogue of interesting facts. In my second, I showed how this new system could be adopted in Massachusetts, and how it would affect every town, every school, and especially every family in the State; . . . in my third I showed that all these great practical Christian results could be realized *by establishing State Normal Schools,* and could not be realized without them, and therefore the proposed school-reform must begin with introducing such Normal Schools."

Brooks opened his campaign with a sermon which he preached in his own church at Hingham. Here he made the statement: "From what I have learned, it is now my opinion that the Prussian system is to make a new era in the public education of the United States." He then sent out circulars to the selectmen, school committees, clergymen and other citizens of Plymouth County inviting them to a meeting in Plymouth where he would speak on the need of teachers' seminaries. The meeting was a great success, one substantial citizen at once pledging $1000 for a teachers' seminary in Plymouth County. "Thus my client, the Prussian stranger, began its journey from the Plymouth Rock." (P. 8.)

For three years Brooks traveled up and down the State of Massachusetts lecturing on the Prussian normal schools in churches, lyceums and before teachers' conventions. In 1837 the legislature established the State Board of Education which, as everybody knew, meant the establishment of state normal schools. In the following year these were adopted by statute. Brooks closes the account of his labors with the words: "I say it was the Prussian system which wrought out the educational regeneration of New England." (P. 12.)

Brooks had also drawn up the petition of the Convention held at Halifax in Plymouth County, January, 1837, asking the Legislature of Massachusetts for the establishment of normal schools. Here we read: "The Prussian system, better than any with which we are acquainted, aims at unfolding the whole nature of man as the Creator designed; thus bringing out all the talent of the country, and thereby giving to every child the chance of making the most of himself. . . . The Prussian system, therefore, is emphatically a Christian system."[14a]

The fame of the Prussian school system also penetrated to the South. In 1838, Dr. Benjamin M. Smith, prominent in the public school movement of Virginia, submitted to Governor David Campbell of Virginia, at the Governor's request, certain "observations on the system of education pursued in some European countries which may be useful to the General Assembly of our own State." It was a report on the Prussian Primary School System followed by a supplement, "Suggestions on the Application of this System of Primary Schools to Virginia." Smith had spent some time in Prussia. His report is based on "notes taken on the spot and the observations of others under similar circumstances, particularly Professor Stowe of Cincinnati." In his supplement he states: "We cannot copy such a monarchical system, but we can catch certain principles for application in a republic." He deduces five principles from the Prussian system: first, education is a state and parental duty; second, the principle of general taxation for schools, "we must see that education is a public benefit and tax ourselves for it"; third, Prussian success is largely due to trained teachers; a normal department should be established at each college; fourth, we might imitate the superior machinery of the Prussian schools; fifth, more science, civil government, and good citizenship, drawing, and agriculture should be introduced. His last recommendation goes beyond the Prussian system: "he demonstrates the practical necessity of having a *free* system from primary to university for every child."[14b]

The work of Charles Brooks was continued by Horace Mann, who as secretary of the Board of Education of the State of Massachusetts for twelve years (1837-48) left his impress upon the public schools of his State and his country. During his secretaryship the first State Normal School after the German model was opened in Lexington, Massachusetts, in 1839. At the end of each year Horace Mann published a report on his official activity. We have twelve such reports, the most important being the seventh, in which he gives an account of what he saw in Germany and other European countries during a five months' educational trip through Europe in 1843. To the Prussian schools he devotes most attention. "Among the nations of Europe," he writes,[15] "Prussia has long enjoyed the most distinguished reputation for the excellence of its schools. In reviews, in speeches, in tracts and even in graver works devoted to the cause of education, its schools have been exhibited as models for the imitation of the rest of Christendom." He mentions the attacks upon the Prussian school system made by the popular English traveler Laing[16] but he does not believe that Laing ever actually visited a Prussian school. The school-houses and especially the ventilation of the school-rooms he finds inferior to what he has seen in Massachusetts (pp. 266, 268), but he is deeply impressed with the quality of the Prussian teachers and the range of subjects taught in the common schools, the thoroughness and coherence of the teaching. "The Prussian teacher uses no book," he writes (p. 342), "he needs none. He teaches from a full mind. He cumbers and darkens the subject with no technical phraseology. He observes what proficiency the child has made, and then adapts his instruction both in quality and amount, to the necessity of the case. . . . He connects the subject of each lesson with all kindred and collateral ones, and shows its relations to the every-day duties and business of life." "As a body of men their character is more enviable than that of either of the three so-called 'professions.' They have more benevolence and self-sacrifice than the legal and medical, while they have less of sanctimoniousness and austerity . . . than the clerical." (P. 351.)

Horace Mann places Prussia and the other states of the Germanic Confederation at the head of

European countries in matters pertaining to education. The best hand-writing he has seen in the Prussian schools. "I can hardly express myself too strongly on this point," he writes (p. 327). "In Great Britain, France, or in our own country, I have never seen any schools worthy to be compared with theirs in this respect."

The objection made again and again in America that the introduction of Prussian methods of instruction and of the preparation of teachers would open the door for the coming in of Prussian despotism, he brushes aside as bigoted and worthless. "If the Prussian school-master has better methods of teaching reading, writing, grammar, geography, arithmetic, etc., so that, in half the time he produces greater and better results, surely we may copy his modes of teaching these elements, without adopting his notions of passive obedience to government, or of blind adherence to the articles of a church." (P. 241.) "If Prussia can pervert the benign influences of education to the support of arbitrary power, we surely can employ them for the support and perpetuation of republican institutions. . . . Besides, a generous and impartial mind does not ask whence a thing comes, but what it is. Those who, at the present day, would reject an improvement because of the place of its origin, belong to the same school of bigotry with those who inquired if any good could come out of Nazareth." (P. 242.)

In this connection it may be interesting to recall a prediction that Horace Mann made in the same report. "No one who witnesses that quiet, noiseless development of mind which is now going forward in Prussia, through the agency of its educational institutions, can hesitate to predict that the time is not far distant when the people will assert their right to a participation in their own government." (P. 378.) It was only five years later that the revolution of 1848 took place. A similar opinion was expressed by an intelligent American woman, Miss Catherine Maria Sedgwick, who traveled in Germany in 1840. In her *Letters from Abroad*[17] she writes: "It is impossible to witness the system of general instruction in Germany without asking if the rulers are not making an experiment dangerous to the maintenance of absolutism."

The last comprehensive work of this period dealing with European education was published in 1854 by Henry Barnard, at the time Superintendent of Common Schools in Connecticut, entitled *National Education in Europe*.[18] The volume contains 890 pages, more than one-third being devoted to the schools of

Germany. It is based upon Barnard's own observations during a stay in Germany in 1835-36 and upon the publications of Stowe, Bache, Horace Mann, and an Englishman, Joseph Kay,[19] who in 1850 had published a most favorable account of the German school system. I quote the introductory paragraph of Barnard's work: "To Germany . . . belongs the credit of first thoroughly organizing a system of public education under the administration of the civil power. Here, too, education first assumed the form and name of a science, and the art of teaching and training children was first taught systematically in seminaries established for this special purpose."

Henry Barnard and Horace Mann were the two great leaders in the Common School Revival of the middle of the nineteenth century.

When we examine the volumes of the educational journals published in the United States from the thirties to the latter part of the nineteenth century, especially the *American Journal of Education* (1856-81) edited by Henry Barnard, we are impressed with the large number of translations from German educational works, with the many accounts of German methods of instruction and the training of teachers, and with the general interest in everything pertaining to German schools and German teachers.

In a notice of a German Reader that had just been published in Boston in connection with Follen's German Grammar, the *American Journal and Annals of Education and Instruction,* in its first issue of 1831 (p. 550), points out the great value of the German language, which is called "the noblest of modern languages," and continues: "We earnestly hope these books may excite an additional attention to this rich mine of theory and experiments in education which has so long been neglected among us." Calvin E. Stowe in his essay on *Normal Schools and Teachers' Seminaries,* (Boston, 1839, p. 108), also recommended the study of German to all teachers: "The rich abundance and variety of educational literature in this language greater, I venture to say, than in all other languages together, render it an acquisition of the highest importance to every teacher."

Hinsdale, in his *Life of Horace Mann,* has summed up the influence of the German schools as follows (p. 299): "From an early period in the history of the Common School Revival, German influence has been steady, strong and wholesome. It has been derived from the introduction of German pedagogical literature, from the frequent visits of our pedagogists and teachers to German schools, from the attendance of our scholars upon German universities, and the not inconsiderable number of German teachers who have found employment on this side of the Atlantic."

About the middle of the century a new movement came from Germany deeply affecting the education of very young children and adding a new word to the vocabulary of American English, Froebel's kindergarten. The kindergarten according to Froebel was to be not merely a place for the supervision of children not old enough to go to school, but it was to develop and strengthen their bodies by appropriate games and exercises; it was to train their senses and to occupy their awakening minds, to make them acquainted with nature and man, to instill into them a sense of social obligations which the home with its isolation could not give; it was to give them religious training suited to their immature minds and to develop all their faculties harmoniously by setting free their inborn gifts and powers, just as the plant in the garden develops from within when given proper care.

The first to make the American public acquainted with the ideas of the kindergarten was a German, Johannes Kraus, a personal disciple of Froebel and an ardent advocate of the new movement, who came to this country in 1851. By lectures and articles written for the press he called attention to the ideas of Froebel. Henry Barnard, the first United States Commissioner of Education (1867-70), invited him to become associated with the United States Bureau of Education. Kraus accepted, as this gave him the opportunity of promoting his kindergarten ideas on a national scale.[20]

Henry Barnard had become interested in Froebel's system when, as American delegate, he attended the International Exhibit of Educational Systems and Materials held at London in 1854, which included the whole material of Froebel's kindergarten. In his report to the Governor of Connecticut he referred to this system and to its application by Madame Ronge, as he had seen it in her kindergarten in Tavistock Square, London, as "by far the most original, attractive and philosophical form of infant development the world has yet seen."[21] At the fourth session of the American Association for the Advancement of Education held at Washington, December, 1854, he delivered an address on the subject, and in his *American Journal of Education* he described the exhibits of kindergarten material he had seen in London. (*Journal*, vol. I, p. 8, and II, pp. 449-451 (1855 and '56).

The first practical application of Froebel's kindergarten idea in the United States was made by Mrs. Carl Schurz, the wife of the well-known German-American statesman, at Watertown, Wisconsin, in 1856. The event was commemorated at Watertown in 1929 by the dedication of a tablet to the memory of Mrs. Carl Schurz, "who established on this site the first kindergarten in America, 1856."[22] Mrs. Schurz, Margaret Meyer before her marriage, had taken a course of lectures with Froebel at Hamburg, her former home. She had gone to England to aid her sister, Madame Ronge, who had established the first kindergartens in England at Manchester and London and had prepared the exhibit that aroused the admiration of Dr. Barnard. In her new home at Watertown, Wisconsin, Mrs. Schurz opened a private kindergarten for her little daughter and the children of some relatives and neighbors. The second kindergarten, also German, was established by Miss Caroline L. Frankenberg in Columbus, Ohio. Miss Frankenberg had taught in Froebel's institute at Keilhau before he had developed in full his kindergarten system. She kept an infant school in Columbus, Ohio, in 1836, but soon returned to Germany, where she again taught for a number of years in Froebel's school. Upon her return to the United

States she opened a kindergarten after Froebel's new system at Columbus, Ohio, in 1853, two years after the kindergarten of Mrs. Schurz.[23] Of the ten kindergartens established in the United States before 1870, all except one were conducted by Germans. They were found in the cities with a considerable German population usually in connection with the bilingual schools established by the Germans. They prepared the way for the general acceptance of the kindergarten idea.[24]

The *Christian Examiner* (Boston) of 1859 (pp. 313-339), gave a lengthy and appreciative account of Froebel's system in a review of three works that had appeared in England and Belgium, *Les Jardins d'Enfants*, Brussels and Ostend, 1858, by Baroness von Marenholtz-Bülow, the same lady's *Woman's Educational Mission*, London, 1855, and Johannes and Bertha Ronge's *A Practical Guide to the English Kindergarten*, London, 1855. The two last named books were also highly praised in an article on "Infant Gardens" that appeared in the London magazine *Household Words*, edited by Charles Dickens, July 21, 1855.

In 1859 Mrs. Schurz met Miss Elizabeth Palmer Peabody at the home of a mutual friend at Roxbury, now a part of Boston. It was through Mrs. Schurz that Miss Peabody heard for the first time of Froebel's kindergarten, and in Mrs. Schurz's little daughter, who greatly impressed Miss Peabody with her naturalness, intelligence and exemplary behavior she saw the results of kindergarten training. Miss Peabody has herself given an account of this meeting.[25] Mrs. Schurz later sent her a part of Froebel's book, *The Education of Man.* The reading of this book, Mrs. Schurz's explanations, and the results of such training as exemplified in the little girl, inspired Miss Peabody, who was an experienced teacher, with the greatest enthusiasm for the new system of education. In the following year, 1860, she opened the first kindergarten in Boston. After a few years, however, she realized that she had been conducting a successful infant school rather than a kindergarten in the manner of Froebel. To learn the real kindergarten methods she decided in 1867 to go to Germany to study at the source.

During her absence her sister, Mrs. Horace Mann, invited a German kindergartener, Mrs. Matilda R. Kriege, and her daughter, Alma, who had been conducting for a few months a kindergarten in New York in connection with a German school, to come to Boston to take charge of Miss Peabody's kindergarten. Both ladies had received their training in the school of Baroness von Marenholtz-Bülow at Berlin; the latter during the last years of Froebel and after his death had become the great apostle of kindergarten training throughout Europe. Mrs. Kriege and her daughter also opened the first kindergarten training school in Boston in 1868.[26]

In 1872 Miss Maria Boelte came to New York at the invitation of the principal of a large private school for girls and opened a kindergarten in connection with the school. Miss Boelte belonged to a distinguished and highly cultivated family in Mecklenburg-Schwerin, she had studied with Froebel's widow in Hamburg and had taught kindergarten in Germany and in England.[27] In 1873 she married Johannes Kraus and the two spent their lives in the cause of the kindergarten. They established in New York a training school for kindergartners which for many years was the leading institution of the kind in the country. The *Dictionary of American Biography* characterizes her work and personality with the words: "A woman of unusual personal charm she left an indelible stamp on education in America."

But to Elizabeth Palmer Peabody, more than to any other person, belongs the distinction of having convinced American educators and the American public of the value of the kindergarten method. Upon her return from Germany in 1863, she devoted the rest of her life to the cause of kindergarten education in America by teaching in kindergartens, but still more by writing and lecturing on the subject.

In 1870 the first public kindergarten in America was opened in Boston but it continued only for a few years as the city was not willing to appropriate the necessary funds. The most important step in the history of the kindergarten in America was taken in 1873 by the school board of the city of St. Louis, which, upon the recommendation of the superintendent of the St. Louis public schools, W. T. Harris, later U. S. Commissioner of Education, voted to establish a public kindergarten and to make it a part of the public school system of the city.[28] Under the skillful management of Miss Susan E. Blow the kindergarten proved a great success. Miss Blow had studied with Mrs. Krause-Boelte in New York, later she also studied in Germany with Baroness von Marenholtz-Bülow. From St. Louis the kindergarten idea spread throughout the West. Nowhere, not even in Germany, did it become so firmly rooted as in the United States. This development accords with the statement, somewhat faultily worded, which Miss Peabody attributes to Froebel, that "the spirit of the American nationality was the only one in the world with which his creative method was in complete harmony, and to which the legitimate institutions would present no barriers."[29]

Cousin's Report and the Prussian school system had a decisive influence upon the whole system of public education in the State of Michigan. At the convention that was to frame a constitution for the new State of Michigan, held at Detroit, in 1835, the chairman of the Committee on Education, Isaac E. Crary, was thoroughly familiar with Cousin's Report. He had previously discussed it in detail with his friend and fellow townsman, John D. Pierce, and both had agreed that the constitution of the new State should contain similar provisions.[30] Crary succeeded in getting the convention to adopt the plan thought out and formulated by himself and his friend. John D. Pierce was later appointed Superintendent of Public Instruction, the first state superintendent in the United States. In his work, *The System of Public Instruction and Primary School Law of Michigan,* he states: "The System of Public Instruction which was intended to be established by the framers of the constitution, the conception of the office, its province, its powers and duties were derived from Prussia. That system consisted of three degrees. Primary instruction, corresponding to our district schools; secondary instruction, communicated in schools called Gymnasia; and the highest instruction, communicated in Universities. The superintendence of this entire system, which was formed in 1819, was entrusted to a Minister of State, called the Minister of Public Instruction, and embraced everything which belonged to the moral and intellectual advancement of the people. The system of Michigan was intended to embrace all institutions which had for their object the instruction of youth, comprising the education of the primary, the intermediate class of schools, however denominated, and the University." This statement of Superintendent Pierce was quoted with full approbation by the first permanent president of the University of Michigan, Henry P. Tappan, in a discourse delivered on the occasion of his inauguration as Chancellor of the University of Michigan in 1852.[31]

Burke A. Hinsdale, in his *History of the University of Michigan,* makes this comment: "It is no exaggeration to say that a single copy of M. Victor Cousin's Report, which found its way into the oak openings of Michigan, produced results, direct and indirect, that far surpass in importance the results produced by any other educational volume in the whole history of the country."[32]

John D. Pierce is the founder of the public school system of Michigan. His model in the formulation of his duties as Superintendent of Public Instruction was the Prussian minister of instruction.[33] When his office was belittled at the constitutional convention of 1850 he defended himself and his office by saying: "Why is it that Prussia stands at the head of education in Europe? For the simple reason she has a Minister of Public Instruction to superintend and foster everything relating to the education of her people."[34]

In the practical application of the Prussian system, however, it was found that many modifications were necessary to make the system workable in a new country. Moreover, lack of funds prevented the execution of some of the plans. But "it has been the boast of the state that her system of public instruction is based on 'the Prussian idea,' the idea that the state should create, support and supervise a system of free public instruction, comprehending the three grades, elementary schools, secondary schools, and the university. The constitution of the State, framed in 1835, incorporated these ideas in outline."[35]

The University of Michigan is the first institution of higher learning in this country avowedly based, in theory at least, upon the German model. It followed at first the German custom of having the president elected annually by the faculty. That was also the practice of the University of Virginia down to 1905. It has been suggested that Thomas Jefferson may have gotten the idea from the German universities,[36] but it is far more likely that Jefferson's inborn aversion to all permanent concentration of power in the hands of one man, his ardent devotion to the republican form of government, induced him to establish a rotating chairmanship instead of a permanent presidency. At Michigan, as later at Virginia, it was found that this German practice did not work in American institutions, and both universities, Michigan after a few years, adopted the American practice of electing permanent presidents.

The first permanent president of the University of Michigan, Henry Philip Tappan, a man of unusual power, was a great admirer of the German system of education. He had been in Germany and was thoroughly familiar with German educational methods. He came to Michigan with ideals quite in harmony with those of Crary and Pierce, and he believed that these ideals could be carried into practice. The year before entering upon the presidency, in 1851, he had published a volume on *University Education.* Here he writes (p. 39): "In Protestant Germany what an advance has been made! In no part of the world has University education been so enlarged, and made so liberal and thorough. The Universities of Protestant Germany stand forth as model institutions, if there be such to be found; and the whole system of education, from the Common School upward, exhibits an intellectual progress which commands our admiration."[37] Of the system as a whole he says (p. 45): "The Educational System of Germany and particularly in Prussia, is certainly a very noble one. We cannot well be extravagant in its praise. Thorough in all its parts, consistent with itself, and vigorously sustained, it furnishes every department of life with educated men, and keeps up at the Universities themselves, in every branch of knowledge, a supply of erudite and elegant scholars and authors, for the benefit and glory of the country, and the good of mankind." Tappan clearly saw the shortcomings of the Prussian government. In the account of his travels through Europe[38] he deprecates the illiberal methods of the Prussian government but, he adds, "we must be just. In the educational system of Prussia we have something more than theory. Here is a glorious achievement of an enlightened and energetic despotism."

In his inaugural address delivered at Ann Arbor in December, 1852, Tappan emphasizes the common educational standard of Prussia and Michigan. "Prussia and Michigan are examples of States creating educational systems. The first has been completely successful, and the institutions of Prussia, like ancient learning and art, stand before us as models which we are constrained to admire, to approve and to copy. The institutions of Michigan are yet in their infancy, but we think there is the promise of a bright career, of a full and ripe development, which cannot well disappoint us." Later in the address he says: "Michigan has the credit of proclaiming the Prussian model. She has wisely adopted the most perfect standard as her standard. Let us see how far she has already conformed to it." He then proceeds to explain why Michigan through force of circumstances has not yet secondary schools like the gymnasia nor a university like the Prussian universities.[39]

In a discourse on *The Progress of Educational Development* delivered in 1855, Tappan returned to his favorite subject.[40] After giving an historical sketch of the progress of education he continues: "We have thus, in pursuing the course of educational development, been led to the German, or, as it is more commonly called, to the Prussian system, its highest and most perfect representative in modern times. We have been led to this inevitably. It is not the opinion of an individual, or of a class; it is the conclusion of a demonstration; or rather it is an obvious fact, which only the grossest ignorance or the most stupid prejudice could presume to deny. The wisest philosophers and the greatest educators have united in commending this system." As his authorities, "were it necessary to appeal to authority," he says he might mention Cousin of France and Sir William Hamilton of Scotland, who had reviewed Cousin's Report in the *Edinburgh Review* and had expressed his great admiration for the educational system of Prussia. Near the end of the discourse Tappan sums up Michigan's educational debt to Prussia: "Throughout the legislation of our State on the subject of education, in the plans of education drawn up by our wisest and best men, in our constitutional provisions, and in the forms of institutions which have been attempted, or which have attained a permanent existence, we find the Prussian system announced as a model and more or less developed. Our primary schools, our Normal school, our superintendent of public instruction are directly copied from Prussia." The first catalogue of the University

(1852-53) issued during his presidency contained the statement: "The State of Michigan has copied from Prussia what is acknowledged to be the most perfect educational system in the world."[41]

Tappan was frequently attacked by the newspapers of the State and by super-patriots for his "Prussian" policy, even members of the legislature resenting his repeated references to his German educational prototypes,[42] but he imparted to the University of Michigan a breadth of spirit which soon made the young institution a leader in higher education. James B. Angell, who became president of the University in 1871, was impressed with the spirit of the University. In his *Reminiscences*[43] he writes: "I found (in coming to Ann Arbor) that largely under the influence of John D. Pierce, Superintendent of Public Instruction at the time of its organization, of Isaac E. Crary and of Henry P. Tappan, its first President, the University had been inspired to a considerable extent by German ideals of education and was shaped under broader and more generous views of university life than most of the eastern colleges."

Michigan's school system, and especially its university, served as model for many of the Western States.

fifty

The influence of German universities upon higher education in the United States has been profound.[44] It began later than the influence of the German common schools but it continued down to recent times. The nineteenth century was the great period of German universities. They had developed the conception of *akademische Freiheit,* academic freedom, which in its full sense did not exist anywhere else. Academic freedom applied to professors and students alike. For the students it meant that they were free to choose their studies and that they were masters of their own lives. For the professors it meant that they were secure in their positions and that they were free to teach what they believed to be the truth. Neither the Church nor the State nor outmoded tradition nor political parties were to interfere with their studies and investigations. This academic freedom was the palladium of the German universities and there are comparatively few instances where it was violated. Academic freedom, more than any other factor, made the German universities the center of progressive thought in investigations of every kind. They attracted students from every country in the world but from nowhere more than from the United States. American students found in Germany what their own country was still lacking, the most advanced scientific methods, independence of thought and investigation, love and unselfish devotion to science and learning. The high position that American scholarship occupies today, the leading position it holds in some branches of knowledge, are due directly and indirectly to the many Americans who got their advanced training and their inspiration at German universities. From the seventies of the last century down to the second decade of our century there were several hundred Americans every year studying at German institutions of higher learning.

At the fiftieth Convocation of the University of Chicago held in March 1904, Professor John M. Coulter delivered an address, *The Contributions of Germany to Higher Education,* in which he did full justice to the debt that American universities and American scholarship owe to the German universities.[45]

It was only natural that American students upon their return from Germany should introduce German methods and the spirit of German scholarship into American universities, transforming some of the older colleges into real universities. Postgraduate courses were established which later developed into graduate schools where the methods of instruction were no longer the school methods of the old college but the advanced methods of the German universities. The lecture system came to be widely used. Emphasis was placed on research and original investigation. The seminar, that characteristic invention of German universities, was introduced: professor and advanced students meet to discuss problems and to find a solution. The student does the work, the professor lends a guiding hand. It is the training ground for original scholarship. What was probably the first seminar in an American university was the one held by Professor Charles Kendall Adams in history at the University of Michigan in 1871.[46]

Today there is not a graduate school in the country that does not have its seminars or, at least, courses where the method, if not the name, is employed. The German degree of Doctor of Philosophy, which has nothing to do with philosophy in the accepted sense, was introduced. It is the degree which in German universities is granted by the faculty of philosophy, that one of the four medieval university faculties to which in Germany all the new studies and sciences were added which in modern times have become a part of university instruction. The degree of Ph.D., in spite of much opposition and ridicule, has become so firmly established in American academic life that in many places it is almost a *sine qua non* of an academic position. Harvard granted its first Ph.D. degree in 1873, Michigan in 1876.

With the founding of the Johns Hopkins University at Baltimore in 1876, America had for the first time a university that represented the type of the German universities not only in theory but in reality. Though Johns Hopkins also had a collegiate department, the emphasis was placed from the very beginning upon advanced work, upon the university character of the new institution. Johns Hopkins was indeed intended to be an American university, not a German university, but to quote the words of Fabian Franklin, the biographer of Daniel Coit Gilman, founder and first president of the new university, "It may be said with sufficient accuracy that the graduate work was carried on in its main lines upon the model of the German universities. . . . The keynote of the German system was also the keynote of Mr. Gilman's conception of the university that was to be." "The vital force of the University was directed in the main to the building up in America of a true university, a university permeated by the spirit of the universities of Germany, with research as the center, the heart, of the whole organism."[47] In an article in the *Nation* published October 22, 1908, after President Gilman's death, Dr. Franklin writes: "It was, of course, in

the main, the adoption of German university stand-
ards and methods that characterized the new university at Baltimore, and differentiated it from anything that had theretofore existed in America." From
the founding of the Johns Hopkins University "will
always be dated the raising of America's chief institutions of learning to the plane of real universities, and
indeed the beginning in our country of productive
intellectual activity on a large scale in the higher
fields of research."[48]

On this last point we also have the testimony of
two of the best known American university presidents.
At the twenty-fifth anniversary of the founding of
Johns Hopkins University, President Harper of
Chicago said in his address: "During this first period
the Johns Hopkins University has been the most
conspicuous figure in the American university world,
and to its achievements we are largely indebted for
the fact that we now enter upon a higher mission."
And President Eliot of Harvard said on the same
occasion: "I want to testify that the Graduate School
of Harvard University, started feebly in 1870 and
1871, did not thrive until the example of Johns
Hopkins forced our faculty to put their strength into
the development of our instruction for graduates.
And what was true of Harvard was true of every

other university in the land which aspired to create an advanced school of arts and sciences."[49]

German literature outside of the educational and scholarly fields has not had so pronounced an influence on American culture and education, but there has been more influence than is generally assumed. A number of studies have appeared in recent years, especially at the University of Wisconsin, that show the large number of translations from the German that appeared in American magazines and periodicals during a good part of the nineteenth century. They show a wide interest in German literature, especially of the classical period, and a considerable knowledge of it. Among the German works of the nineteenth century that are mentioned or translated we miss the dramas of men like Kleist, Grillparzer, Otto Ludwig, Hebbel, we miss the novels of men like Gottfried Keller or Konrad Ferdinand Meyer, the writers whom the Germans themselves consider representative of their literature in the nineteenth century after Goethe. What we find are the works of lesser men, lyrics, stories of tenderness and homely virtues, moralizing tales, the type of literature that Americans of that day were fond of and that they cultivated themselves.[50] But there are two places and periods in the history of American culture where

German literature for a time was a vital factor. They are New England and the transcendental movement in the middle of the nineteenth century, and St. Louis in the Middle West and the St. Louis movement in philosophy in the period following the Civil War.

Transcendentalism, in the words of William Ellery Channing, one of its founders,[51] "was an assertion of the inalienable integrity of man, of the immanence of Divinity in instinct. In part, it was a reaction against Puritan Orthodoxy, in part, an effect of renewed study of the ancients, of oriental Pantheists, of Plato and the Alexandrians, of Plutarch's morals, Seneca and Epictetus; in part a natural product of the culture of the place and time. On the somewhat stunted stock of Unitarianism . . . had been grafted German idealism, as taught by the masters of most various schools, — by Kant and Jacobi, Fichte and Novalis, Schelling and Hegel, Schleiermacher and De Wette, by Madame de Staël, Cousin, Coleridge, Carlyle; and the result was a vague yet exalting conception of the godlike nature of the human spirit."

The influence of German philosophy upon the whole transcendental movement was brought out clearly in an article by two Princeton professors,

J. W. Alexander and Albert B. Dod, published in the *Princeton Review* in 1839 and republished by Andrews Norton at Cambridge in 1840. It bore the title, *Concerning the Transcendental Philosophy of the Germans and of Cousin and Its Influence on Opinion in This Country*. It was published together with an article on *The School of Hegel* by Charles Hodge which had also first appeared in the *Princeton Review*. Both articles are opposed to the transcendental philosophy on account of its pantheistic tendencies. Pantheism, in the opinion of the authors, is merely the latest form of infidelity. Cousin is to them the propounder of German ideas. "If we are to make experiment of a new system, we would fain have it fully and fairly before our eyes, which can never be the case so long as we receive our *philosophemata* by a double transportation, from Germany via France, in parcels to suit the importers; as fast as the French forwarding philosopher gets it from Germany, and as fast as the American consignee can get it from France. There is a great inconvenience in the reception of philosophical theories by installments; and if our cisatlantic metaphysicians import the German article we are sometimes forced to wait until they have learned the language well enough to hold a decent colloquy in it. Such, however, is precisely the disadvantage under which the young philosophers of America now labor. . . . Some of them are busily learning French, in order to read in that language any *rifacimento* of Teutonic metaphysics which may come into their hands. Some are learning German; others have actually learned it. He who cannot do either, strives to gather into one the Sibylline oracles and abortive scraps of the gifted but indolent Coleridge, and his gaping imitators; or in default of all this, sits at the urn of dilute wisdom, and sips the thrice drawn infusion of English from French, and French from German." (Pp. 10, 11, 33.) In Emerson's address delivered before the Senior Class in Divinity at Harvard University (July 15, 1838) the authors see "another alarming symptom" of the progress of this philosophy in America. (P. 66.) The impact of the German ideas was disturbing. "It produced some confusion when Leibnitz, Spinoza, Kant, Goethe, Herder, Schleiermacher and Jean Paul came sailing all at once into Boston harbor and discharged their freight."[52]

The New England transcendentalists were less abstract than the Germans and they had more of the missionary spirt. They wanted men to live new lives in accordance with their new light. Hence, they were reformers as well as thinkers. They were no slavish imitators, they were too serious and independent to accept anything which they did not themselves approve. They turned to the study of German with great enthusiasm because it opened to them the treasures of thought which they valued the most. There was probably not one among them who did not read German in some fashion, not that they had learned it in school or college but they acquired it by themselves often in mature life. Margaret Fuller began the study of German by herself at the age of twenty-two. Within a year she had read the most important works of Goethe and Schiller as well as other German writers.[53] Theodore Parker, the great divine, found that he must have a knowledge of German as a student of theology and of letters and learned it by himself.[54] In a vigorous article on German literature that appeared in the *Dial* (1841) he pointed out the great value of the German language to any one interested in scholarship and literature. Charles Follen, who taught German at Harvard from 1825-35, helped them, and Frederick Henry Hedge, himself a transcendentalist, who, as a boy, had attended school in Germany, was "a fountain of knowledge in the way of German."[55]

The German author in whom these men and women were especially interested was Goethe. It was not only Goethe's artistry that attracted them but even more, to use the words of James Freeman Clarke, "the larger life which opened upon so many of them, under Goethe's lead."[56] For these men and women lived with ideas, they sought a solution of the riddles of life and that made them turn to Goethe. Goethe never had a more enthusiastic or a more devoted disciple in this country than Margaret Fuller. Emerson said of her: "Nowhere did Goethe find a braver, more intelligent or more sympathetic reader."[57] Goethe's principle of self-culture she made her own and preached it to her friends. It is doubtful if there was anybody in Germany at that time who had a better understanding and a keener appreciation of the great poet. In reply to a fierce and unjust attack upon Goethe by the German critic Wolfgang Menzel she published a noble defense of the poet in the *Dial* (Vol. I, No. 3, 1840), a New England woman defending Goethe against one of his own countrymen! In her *Woman in the Nineteenth Century,* that little book which has been a powerful factor in bringing about the present state of equality of American women, she points to Goethe's women as showing the way. "What woman needs," she writes, "is not as a woman to act or rule, but as a nature to grow, as an intellect to discern, as a soul to live freely and unimpeded, to unfold such powers as were given her when we left our common home." Just that she finds in Goethe's women. "Goethe, proceeding on his own track, elevating the human being, in the most imperfect states of society, by continual efforts at self-culture, takes as good care of women as of men." "He aims at a pure self-subsistence, and a free development of any powers with which women may be gifted by nature, as much for them as for men. They are units, addressed as souls. Accordingly, the meeting between Man and Woman, as represented by him, is equal and noble."[58]

Emerson admired Goethe in many ways. He has said some of the finest things about Goethe but also some of the worst. For at heart the two men were essentially different. Emerson, in spite of his inner freedom and his undogmatic views, could never quite rid himself of the Puritanic idea that this world is a place of sin and the body a vessel of uncleanliness. Goethe believed in the unity of God and nature, he insisted upon the whole of life, but the whole of life includes the good and the beautiful and the joys of life are a part of the good and the beautiful.

The New Englanders of the middle of the nineteenth century were interested in German literature, especially in Goethe and Schiller. The objections they

had to Goethe were summed up by Margaret Fuller
in four terse sentences: "He is not a Christian; he is
not an Idealist; he is not a Democrat; he is not a
Schiller."[59] The statement is indeed the best proof of
their interest in German literature. Goethe was to
them a living force, a matter of personal concern,
whether their attitude was sympathetic, hostile, or
reserved.

John Lothrop Motley published an article on
Goethe's *Faust* in the *New York Review* of 1839
which shows an understanding and a grasp of the
subject hardly rivaled by anything that appeared on
Faust in Germany at the time. No less remarkable
is an article on the second part of Goethe's *Faust*
published by Mrs. Sarah Helen Power Whitman in
the *Boston Quarterly Review* of 1840. It would be
hard to find a German criticism of the second part at
the time that shows such sympathetic understanding,
such humility and such æsthetic enjoyment as this
essay of Mrs. Whitman. To the great German Faust
critic, Friedrich Vischer, her contemporary, the second
part remained throughout his life a stumbling-block
and foolishness.

When James Freeman Clarke wrote the biography
of his friend Margaret Fuller, he could not better
describe her than by comparing her to characters in

Goethe's *Wilhelm Meister* and in *Faust*. "Margaret was to persons younger than herself, a Makaria and Natalia. She was wisdom and intellectual beauty. . . . To those older than herself she was like the Euphorion in Goethe's drama, child of Faust and Helen,— a wonderful union of exuberance and judgment born of romantic fullness and classic limitation."[60] James Freeman Clarke assumed that his readers were familiar with *Wilhelm Meister* and *Faust*.

Goethe, Schiller, German philosophy and literature formed a part of the intellectual life of New England about the middle of the nineteenth century as never before and never since.

The first half of the nineteenth century saw in New England the formation of the Unitarian movement with which the transcendentalists were more or less connected, and within the Unitarian movement a further division into conservatives and radicals. In the theological controversies resulting from this, German theological literature plays a decisive part. The theological journals and the controversial literature of the time are full of articles and references bearing on German theology. Names like D. F. Strauss, DeWette, Schleiermacher, Eichhorn, Paulus, Marheineke, Tholuck, Hengstenberg, representing the most varied theological views from extreme radicalism to strict orthodoxy, are mentioned again and again. They are quoted with approval and disapproval. Theodore Parker was steeped in German theological thought. He translated DeWette's *Introduction to the Old Testament* and carried on a personal correspondence with some of the German theologians. The diary which he kept during his trip in Germany records the visits he paid to his German theological friends. The influence of the German theological thought upon American theology, profound as it was, has never been adequately treated.

When we consider that the transcendental movement, the theological controversies and the Common School Revival were more or less contemporaneous about the middle of the nineteenth century, we may indeed speak of a vitalizing influence of German thought and literature upon American education and culture.

The most significant intellectual and spiritual movement that arose in the Middle West is the so-called St. Louis Movement in Philosophy. It began at the close of the Civil War and lasted till about 1885, when most of its leading members had left St. Louis.[61] Though inspired by German philosophy it is a typical American movement, typical also in the cosmopolitan character of its members. The founder was a German-American, Henry C. Brockmeyer, who had come to this country at the age of seventeen. After working as a bootblack in New York he learned a trade, attended college for a while and finally settled in St. Louis, where he worked as an iron moulder, devoting his free time to study. Later he took up law, went into politics, was elected to the legislature and served one term as lieutenant-governor of the State of Missouri. He is the most picturesque character in the movement. The most distinguished member was William Torrey Harris, a Yankee from Connecticut, teacher and superintendent of schools in St. Louis, later U. S. Commissioner of Education. It was he who recommended to the school board of St. Louis the establishment of a public kindergarten. Another leading member was Thomas Davidson, a Scotchman, who taught in the St. Louis high school. A fourth member and the historian of the movement was Denton J. Snider, a teacher in the public schools, later a lecturer and author of many books. Snider, a graduate of Oberlin College, came from Ohio, but his family was of Southern origin. There were many others connected with the movement, men and women. It began in 1864 with the founding of the Philosophical Society of St. Louis, Brockmeyer being elected president and Harris secretary. The object of the society was the study of speculative philosophy, especially the philosophy of Hegel. It is this society that definitely introduced Hegel's philosophy into the United States. In 1867, Harris founded the *Journal of Speculative Philosophy,* the first metaphysical journal in the country which was to represent German idealistic philosophy, especially the philosophy of Hegel. This interest in German idealistic philosophy suggests the transcendental movement of an earlier period. The journal, which Harris edited for many years, contained translations from German philosophical writers, among them the Hegelian Karl Rosenkranz, also from Goethe, besides original contributions by American scholars.

There was one work of German poetry which made a special appeal to the members of the society on account of its philosophical content, Goethe's *Faust. Faust* was discussed at many of their meetings and all the four leaders have published critical estimates or commentaries on the poem. Their enthusiasm for *Faust* was boundless and they communicated this enthusiasm to the people of St. Louis. Snider reports that for several winters four men delivered lectures on *Faust* in different parts of the city in addition to German lectures on *Faust* in German societies. Even the fashionable ladies of St. Louis organized a Faust club and listened to lectures. *"Faust,* on the whole," says Snider, "may well be called the distinctive poem of the St. Louis Movement—the favorite poem more read and bespoken than any other. Never since has any great work of genius taken such deep and persistent possession of the city's mind. . . . It seemed for a while to express our very consciousness."[62] "Why should St. Louis or a goodly proportion of her thinking people adopt a poem as a kind of spiritual breviary, as an ideal reflector of their very soul-world, making such a book unconsciously into a sort of Literary Bible?" Snider asks.[63] He has an answer truly worthy of an Hegelian philosopher. St. Louis felt an inner relationship between herself and Faust, though she was not clearly conscious of it. Faust has denied the possibility of truth, but if we cannot know the truth, or if what seems such is only a mirage, a lie, then we live in a world of illusion, of untruth, as Faust did. Now St. Louis in those Faust years was living in a world of illusion like Faust. St. Louis's great illusion was the conviction that the city was destined to be the greatest city not only in the West but in the whole United States; yes, her people dreamed of sometime being the center of the inhabited earth. The great illusion was shattered when the census of 1880 showed that Chicago had 150,000 more inhabitants than St. Louis. "Thus for her deepest self-expression, yea for her hope of ultimate salvation, St. Louis adopted as her own this world-poem of Goethe, which thereby became her truly modern and remedial literary Gospel, at least while she lay under her illusory spell."[64]

The Faust publications of the members of the St. Louis Movement all treat Goethe's *Faust* as a work of philosophy and not as a work of poetic art. In analyzing the poem they use the Hegelian method of thesis, antithesis and synthesis. As the poem today is primarily viewed as a work of poetic art and not of philosophy, their treatment has lost much of its original interest. Snider published a Faust commentary in two volumes, the most ambitious Faust work ever attempted in this country, and traveled through the United States lecturing on the poem which was to him one of the literary Bibles of the Occident by the side of Homer, Dante and Shakespeare. Of Faust at the end of the Second Part when he is the ruler of the land which he has reclaimed from the ocean, Snider says: "Faust becomes the settler, the frontiersman on a vast ocean of savagery, he becomes the American, transforming a wild continent into the habitable abode of rational men. Often have we said, much oftener have we thought that this Second Part of *Faust* in many portions seems an American Book, or rather the *Mythus* of America, in its settlement and conquest, as well as in its spiritual significance. That old Europe has not fully appreciated the book, cannot perhaps; but here we can see the mythical forms turning to living facts before our eyes." [65]

The lectures on German philosophy and Goethe initiated by the St. Louis school found favor in other cities. Dr. Harris left St. Louis in 1880. For almost ten years he was connected with the Concord School of Philosophy which had been founded in 1879 by A. Bronson Alcott at Concord, Massachusetts. [66] The Concord School was in session a few weeks every summer. The lectures dealt with philosophy, especially German philosophy, but also with the great representatives of poetic art, Homer, Dante, Shakespeare and the poets of classical antiquity. The session of 1885 was almost entirely devoted to Goethe. The lectures and discussions were published by the secretary of the school, F. B. Sanborn, with the title, *The Life and Genius of Goethe* (Boston, 1886). The success of this Goethe session inspired the Milwaukee Literary School the following summer to offer a similar course of lectures on Goethe. The lectures were published by Marion V. Dudley with the title, *Poetry and Philosophy of Goethe* (Chicago, 1887).

It is a common impression that Goethe never meant much to the spiritual life of America. Not only New England transcendentalism and liberalism but also the St. Louis Movement and the Concord School of Philosophy refute this view. To be sure, these were not popular movements. Philosophy, self-culture and great poetry do not lend themselves to popular movements, but the men and women interested in these movements belonged to the intellectual élite of America.

German influence upon American education and culture during the nineteenth century has been beneficial and profound. It extends to the kindergarten, common schools, normal schools, universities, productive scholarship, and it includes two significant movements in the intellectual and spiritual life of America. The influence of German music has not been touched upon in this sketch. It is not likely that the present century will see anything like it. America has come of age. Moreover, the war and still more the treaty of peace following the war have necessarily brought about changes in Germany that make it impossible to predict what the future development will be. The pride of the German universities, academic freedom, has received a serious blow and we must look to America to uphold that noble tradition. The whole cultural life of Germany has developed a new aspect but the old German idealism is not dead; it is under a partial eclipse and sooner or later will appear again in a new form.

Notes and References

[1] A. B. Faust, *The German Element in the United States.* Boston and New York, 1909, vol. I, p. 145.

[2] *Cf.* D. W. Long, *Literary Pioneers.* Harvard University Press, 1935, where this important aspect of American-German intellectual relations is ably and exhaustively treated.

[3] *Cf.* P. A. Bruce, *History of the University of Virginia.* New York, 1920, vol. I, p. 359, vol. II, p. 65; J. S. Patton, *Jefferson, Cabell and the University of Virginia,* New York, 1906, pp. 86, 96.

[4] *Cf.* Josiah Quincy, *The History of Harvard University.* Boston, 1860, vol. II, pp. 324, 384.

[5] *Cf.* L. Viereck, *Zwei Jahrhunderte Deutschen Unterrichts in den Vereinigten Staaten.* Braunschweig, 1903, p. 12.

[6] *Cf.* Wm. H. Carpenter in *Columbia University Bulletin,* March, 1897, p. 82.

[7] *John D. Pierce. Founder of the Michigan School System. A Study of Education in the Northwest.* By Charles O. Hoyt and R. Clyde Ford, Professors in the State Normal College, Ypsilanti, Michigan. Ypsilanti, Michigan, 1905, p. 17.

[8] *Cf.* Max Lenz, *Geschichte der Königlichen Friedlich-Wilhelms-Universität zu Berlin.* Halle a. S. 1910, vol. I, p. 78.

[9] *Report on Elementary Public Instruction in Europe made to the Thirty-Sixth General Assembly of the State of Ohio.* December 19, 1837. By C. E. Stowe. The Harvard University Library has three early editions of this Report: New York, 1838; Boston, 1838 and 1839, besides later reprints.

[10] *Report on Education in Europe to the Trustees of Girard College for Orphans.* By Alex. Dallas Bache. Philadelphia, 1839.

[11] *American Journal of Education,* vol. IV, p. 14, September, 1857.

[12] *Cf.* J. P. Gordy, *Rise and Growth of the Normal-School Idea in the United States.* Washington, 1891, Bureau of Education, Circular No. 8. Chapter I. V. L. Mangun, *The American Normal School,* Baltimore, 1928, p. 44 ff.

[13] *Cf.* John Albree, *Charles Brooks and his Work for the Normal Schools.* Medford, Mass., 1907. Robert Ulich, *A Sequence of Educational Influences Traced through Unpublished Writings of Pestalozzi, Froebel, Diesterweg, Horace Mann, and Henry Barnard.* Harvard University Press, 1935, p. 44 ff.

[14] Nicolaus Heinrich Julius (1783-1862), born of Jewish parents in Hamburg, later a convert to Roman Catholicism; a physician by profession, distinguished himself through his humanitarian efforts on behalf of prisoners and prison reform. A pure idealist, he devoted his life and his fortune to the improvement of social conditions in Germany. He is the author of *Nordamerikas sittliche Zustände* (1839), a work in two volumes, in which he gives a discriminating account of his studies and observations in the United States from 1834 to 1836. He also translated Ticknor's *History of Spanish Literature,* with additions of his own (1852). There is an appreciative account of his life in the *Allgemeine Deutsche Biographie,* vol. 14, pp. 686-9.

[14a] The petition is reprinted in Barnard's *American Journal of Education,* vol. 18, p. 647 f. *Cf.* also Albree 1. c. p. 18 f.

[14b] *Cf.* W. A. Maddox, *The Free School Idea in Virginia before the Civil War,* New York, 1918, p. 129 ff.

[15] *Annual Reports of the Secretary of the Board of Education of Massachusetts.* Boston, 1891. Report for 1843, p. 240.

[16] Samuel Laing, *Notes of a Traveller on the Social and Political State of France, Prussia, Switzerland, Italy and other parts of Europe, during the Present Century.* London, 1842. An American reprint of the second English edition appeared in Philadelphia in 1846. Laing treats Prussian education in chapters VI, VII and VIII. He paints a rather gloomy picture of conditions in Prussia and Germany. The Prussian school system appears to him conven-

tional and mechanical and a failure so far as the true objects of education are concerned. Compulsory education is to him as abhorrent as compulsory military service.

[17] *Letters from Abroad to Kindred at Home.* By the author of "Hope Leslie," etc. (*i. e.*, Catherine Maria Sedgwick), New York, 1841, p. 224.

[18] *National Education in Europe; being an Account of the Organization, Administration, Instruction and Statistics of Public Schools of different Grades in the Principal States.* By Henry Barnard, LL.D., Superintendent of Common Schools in Connecticut. Second Edition, Hartford, 1854. The first edition, according to the preface, appeared at Hartford in 1851 with the title *Normal Schools and other Institutions, Agencies and Means designed for the Professional Education of Teachers,* but contained only a part of the material of the second edition.

[19] Joseph Kay, an English barrister, published in London in 1850 a work in two volumes entitled *The Social Condition and Education of the People in England and Europe, showing the Results of the Primary Schools and of the Division of Landed Property in Foreign Countries.* The work is based on extensive travels and observations in England and on the Continent. Kay gives a very bright picture of the Prussian schools, many of which he had personally visited. Of the Prussian school teacher he says (vol. II, p. 85): "I felt whenever I was in the company of a Prussian teacher, that I was with a gentleman, whose courteous bearing and intelligent manner of speaking must exert a most beneficial influence upon the peasantry, among whom he lived." Henry Barnard reprinted a part of Kay's comments on Prussian schools in his Journal and later in his book *German Schools and Pedagogy,* New York, 1861, vol. I, pp. 58-64.

[20] *Cf.* H. S. Tarbell, *John Kraus* in *Addresses and Journals of the Proceedings of the National Educational Association,* 1896, pp. 229-30. *Cf.* also *Dictionary of American Biography,* and Nina C. Vandewalker, *The Kindergarten in American Education,* New York, 1908, p. 29.

[21] Henry Barnard, *Papers on Froebel's Kindergarten.* Hartford, 1890, p. 3.

[22] *Cf.* Elizabeth Jenkins, *How the Kindergarten Found Its Way to America. Wisconsin Magazine of History,* vol. 19, No. 1, September, 1930.

[23] *Cf.* Elizabeth Jenkins, l. c. Nina C. Vandewalker, l. c. p. 13.

[24] *Cf.* Nina C. Vandewalker, l. c. p. 13.

[25] *Cf.* Elizabeth P. Peabody, *Origin and Growth of the Kindergarten. Education,* vol. 2 (1881-82), p. 523. *Cf.* also Anne L. Page, *How Elizabeth Peabody Became a Kindergarten Convert. Kindergarten Magazine,* vol. 14 (1901-02), p. 461. Richard G. Boone, *Education in the United States,* New York, 1894, p. 333.

[26] *Cf.* Milton Bradley, *A Successful Man,* published by Milton Bradley Co., Springfield, Mass., 1910, p. 27. Nina C. Vandewalker, l. c. p. 17. Elizabeth P. Peabody, l. c. p. 523 f.

[27] Miss Boelte's *Reminiscences* were published by Henry Barnard in *Kindergarten and Child Culture Papers,* Hartford, 1890, pp. 537-550.

[28] *Cf.* E. G. Dexter, *History of Education in the United States,* New York, 1904, p. 168.

[29] Miss Peabody in Henry Barnard's *Papers on Froebel's Kindergarten,* Hartford, 1890, p. 11.

[30] John D. Pierce himself gave an account of this in a paper read before the Pioneer Society of the State of Michigan. *Cf. Report of the Pioneer Society of the State of Michigan,* vol. I, p. 38 f. Lansing, 1877. *Cf.* also Charles O. Hoyt and R. Clyde Ford, *John D. Pierce, Founder of the Michigan School System,* Ypsilanti, Mich., 1905, p. 3.

[31] *A Discourse Delivered by Henry P. Tappan, D.D., at Ann Arbor, Michigan, on the Occasion of His Inauguration as Chancellor of the University of Michigan,* Dec. 21, 1852. Detroit, 1852, p. 30.

[32] Burke A. Hinsdale, *History of the University of Michigan.* Ed. by Isaac N. Demmon, Ann Arbor, 1906, p. 16.

[33] *Cf.* Charles O. Hoyt and R. Clyde Ford, l. c. p. 121.

[34] *Ibid.,* p. 123.

[35] B. A. Hinsdale, *The Spirit and the Ideals of the University of Michigan. Educational Review,* 1896, p. 359.

[36] *Cf.* J. M. Garnett, *The Elective System of the University of Virginia. Andover Review,* vol. V (1886), p. 362.

[37] Henry P. Tappan, *University Education,* New York, 1851.

[38] Henry P. Tappan, *A Step from the New World to the Old and Back Again,* New York, 1852, vol. II, p. 64.

[39] *A Discourse Delivered by Henry P. Tappan,* etc. Detroit, 1852, pp. 5, 32.

[40] *The Progress of Educational Development. A Discourse Delivered before the Literary Societies of the University of Michigan, June 25, 1855, by Henry P. Tappan, D.D., LL.D., Chancellor of the University.* Ann Arbor, 1855, pp. 3, 4, 42.

[41] B. A. Hinsdale, *History of the University of Michigan.* Ed. by Isaac N. Demmon, Ann Arbor, 1906, p. 86.

[42] Charles M. Perry, *Henry Philip Tappan, Philosopher and University President.* Ann Arbor, 1933, pp. 200, 265. Elizabeth M. Farrand, *History of the University of Michigan,* Ann Arbor, 1885, p. 112.

[43] James B. Angell, *Reminiscences,* New York, 1912, p. 226.

[44] *Cf.* Charles F. Thwing, *A History of Higher Education in America,* New York, 1906, p. 318 f. *Id., The American and the German University,* New York, 1928, *passim.*

[45] *University Records.* University of Chicago, vol. VIII (1904), pp. 348-53.

[46] *Cf.* Elizabeth M. Farrand, l. c. p. 269. B. A. Hinsdale, *The Spirit and the Ideals of the University of Michigan, Educational Review,* 1896, p. 484. F. H. Foster, *The Seminary Method,* New York, 1888, p. 104.

[47] *Cf.* Fabian Franklin, *The Life of Daniel Coit Gilman,* New York, 1910, pp. 196, 227. *Cf.* also Daniel C. Gilman, *The Launching of a University and Other Papers,* New York, 1906, p. 275.

[48] The article is reprinted in a small memorial brochure entitled *Daniel Coit Gilman,* Baltimore, 1908, pp. 48, 52.

[49] *Cf. Johns Hopkins University. Celebration of the Twenty-fifth Anniversary of the Founding of the University and Inauguration of Ira Remsen, LL.D., as President of the University.* Baltimore, 1902, pp. 62, 105.

[50] The numerous references to German literature in one of the leading daily papers of New England have been collected and examined by Camillo von Klenze in an illuminating study; *German Literature in the Boston Transcript,* 1830-1880, *Philological Quarterly,* vol. XI, January, 1931. *Cf.* especially pp. 22-24.

[51] *Memoirs of Margaret Fuller Ossoli,* Boston, 1852, vol. II, p. 12.

[52] *Cf.* C. H. Dall, *Transcendentalism in New England,* Boston, 1897, p. 12.

[53] *Memoirs of Margaret Fuller Ossoli,* Boston, 1852, I, 114.

[54] *Cf.* O. B. Frothingham, *Theodore Parker,* Boston, 1874, p. 28.

[55] *Cf.* T. W. Higginson, *Margaret Fuller Ossoli,* Boston, 1886, p. 44.

[56] *Cf.* James Freeman Clarke, *Autobiography, Diary and Correspondence.* Ed. by E. E. Hale, Boston, 1881, p. 91.

[57] *Cf. Memoirs of Margaret Fuller Ossoli,* Boston, 1852, I, 243.

[58] *Cf. Woman in the Nineteenth Century,* Boston, 1855, pp. 12, 38, 125.

[59] *Cf. Conversations with Goethe Translated from the German of Eckermann*, by S. M. Fuller, Boston, 1839, Preface p. XII.

[60] *Cf. Memoirs of Margaret Fuller Ossoli*, I, 97.

[61] *Cf.* Denton J. Snider, *The St. Louis Movement*. St. Louis, Mo., 1920; Charles M. Perry, *The St. Louis Movement in Philosophy, Some Source Material*. University of Oklahoma Press, 1930. Woodbridge Riley, *American Thought from Puritanism to Pragmatism*, New York, 1915, pp. 240 ff.

[62] Denton J. Snider, l. c. p. 341.

[63] *Ibid.*, p. 344.

[64] *Ibid.*, p. 345.

[65] Denton J. Snider, *Goethe's Faust, Second Part. A Commentary*, Boston, 1886, p. 292.

[66] *Cf.* Austin Warren, *The Concord School of Philosophy. The New England Quarterly*, vol. II, no. 2, 1929.